I'm Reading About WEST VIRGINIA

The Mountain State!

GALLOPADE

by Carole Marsh

Printed and Manufactured in Peachtree City, GA., USA
www.gallopade.com

Book design: John Hanson

Editorial manager: Janice Baker

West Virginia is a great state.

It is one of a kind.

What makes West Virginia special?

Let's read about it and see!

NATIVE AMERICANS

Who lived in West Virginia first?

Native Americans did!

They moved around to find food.
They hunted in West Virginia's woods.
They fished in West Virginia's rivers.
They gathered fruits and seeds and nuts.

EXPLORERS

Explorers came to West Virginia about 350 years ago.
They came from Virginia and other colonies.

The explorers climbed high mountains.
They found many rivers and forests filled with fish and animals.

SETTLEMENT

People from other countries came to West Virginia in the early years. Many of them came from Germany. They called their settlement Mecklenburg. Later, the name was changed to Shepherdstown. It is one of the oldest towns in the state!

West Virginia started out as part of Virginia!

Shepherdstown

STATEHOOD

West Virginia was the 35th state to join the United States of America!

Isn't it great,
to be a state!
I bet West Virginia
could hardly wait!

West Virginia became a state in 1863.

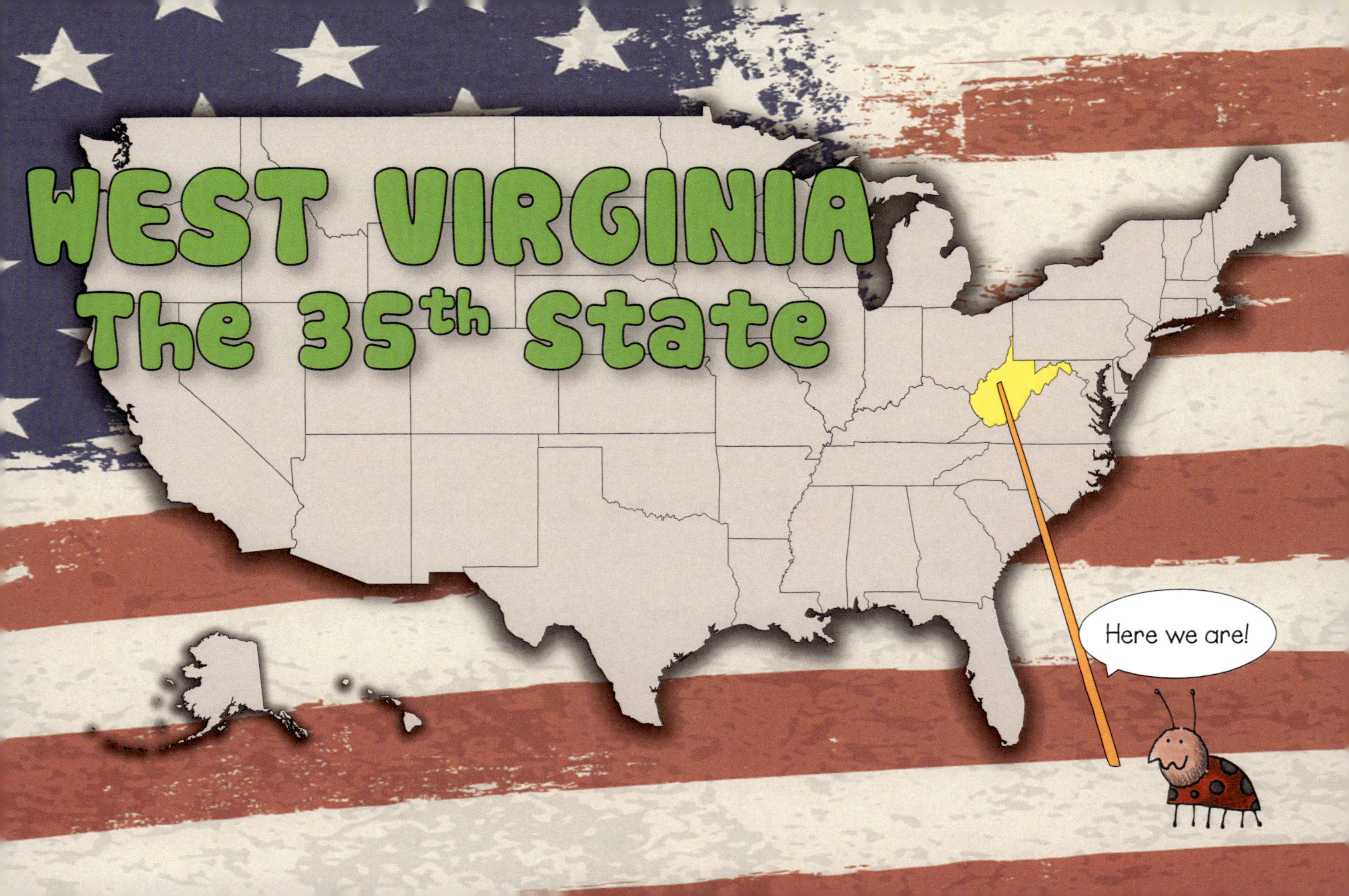
WEST VIRGINIA
The 35th State
Here we are!

FLAG

I am the state flag.
I was adopted in 1929.

What colors am I?
I am blue and white.

Look at me.
What else do you see?

I fly high over the state of West Virginia!

STATE OF WEST VIRGINIA
MONTANI SEMPER LIBERI
JUNE 20 1863

CAPITAL

Say hello to Charleston,
the capital city of West Virginia!

There is an important building in Charleston.
It is the State Capitol.
West Virginia's laws are made there!

Capitol

SEAL

I am a seal,
but I am not the State Seal.
If I were, I would be very important.
I would be stamped on many official papers.
(Ouch, that might hurt!)

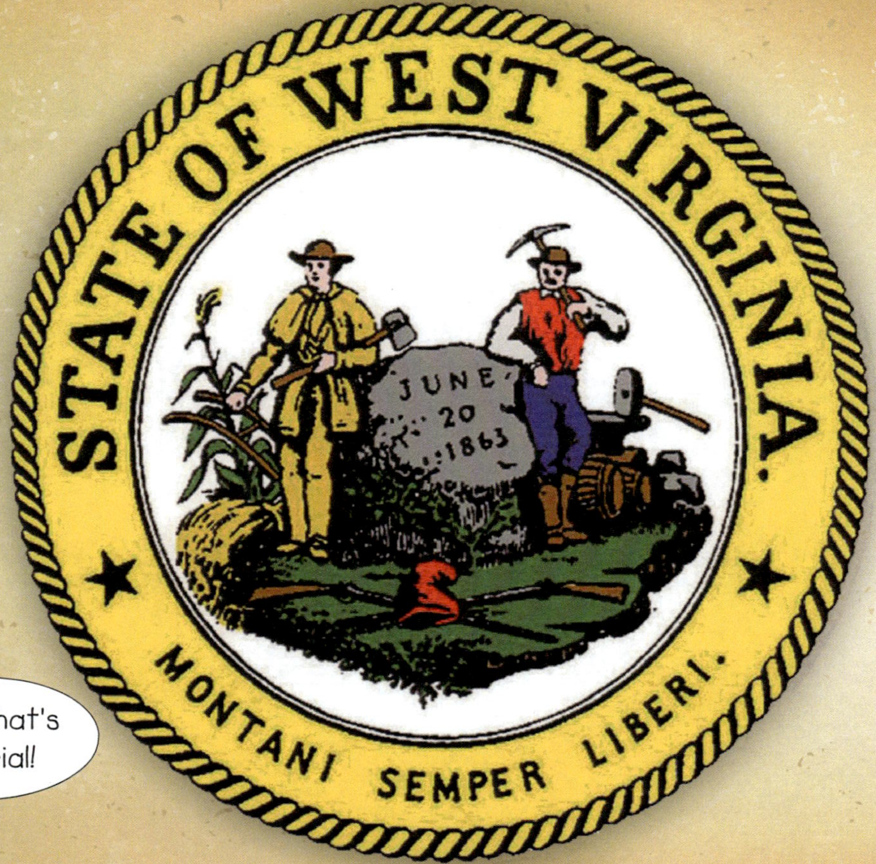
STATE OF WEST VIRGINIA.
JUNE 20 1863
MONTANI SEMPER LIBERI.

Now, that's official!

NICKNAME

State nicknames are fun!
State nicknames are great!
They share fun facts
about each state!

West Virginia's nickname is "The Mountain State."

People love to visit West Virginia's mountains!

The Mountain State

BORDERS

Look at West Virginia.
West Virginia is in a region called "the Mid–Atlantic."

West Virginia borders five other states.
Find them on the map!

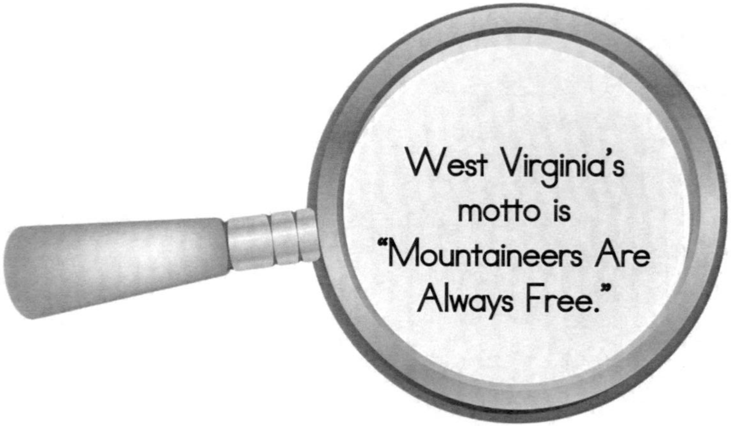

Borders

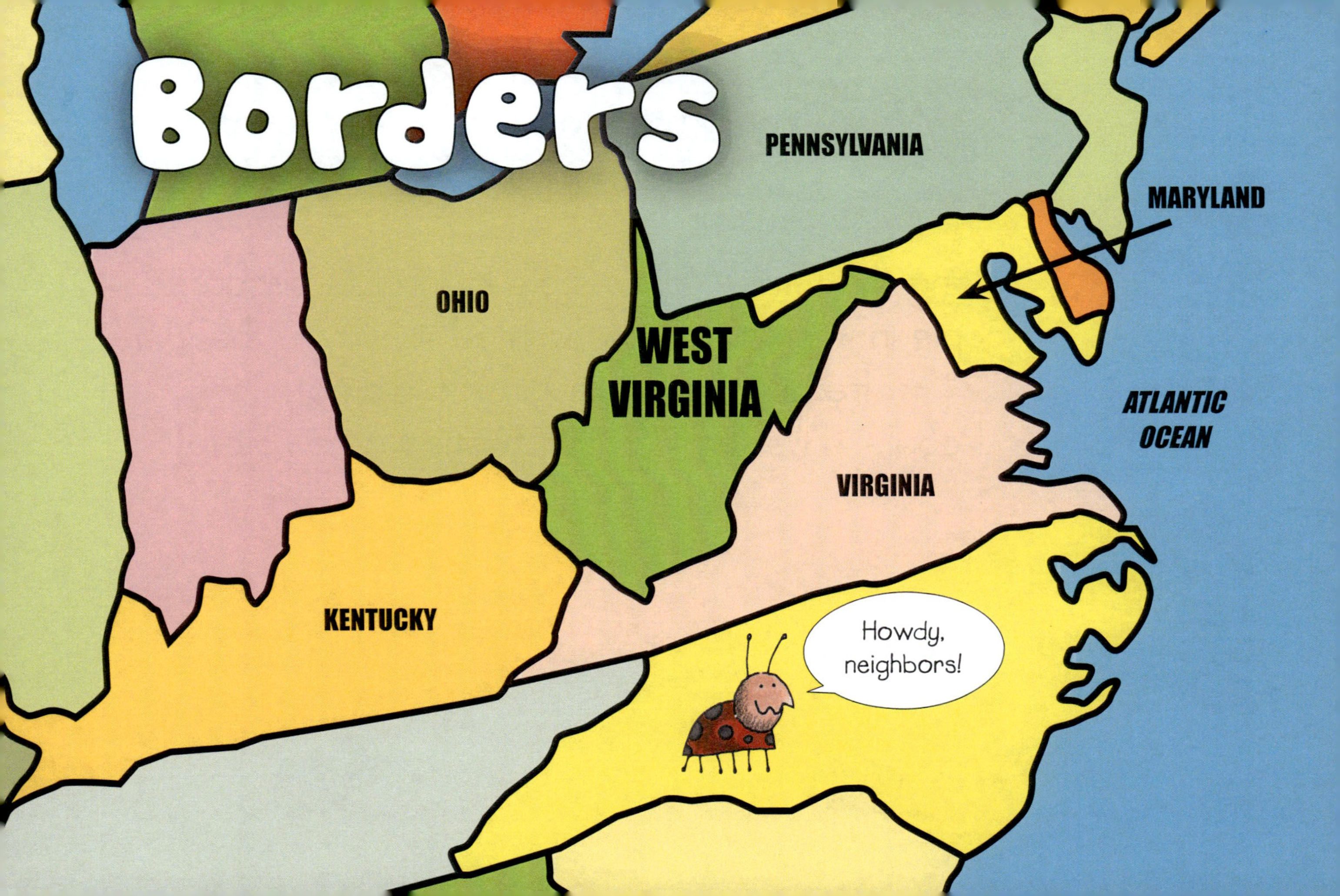

PENNSYLVANIA
MARYLAND
OHIO
WEST VIRGINIA
ATLANTIC OCEAN
VIRGINIA
KENTUCKY
Howdy, neighbors!

HISTORY

West Virginia used to be part of Virginia.
What happened?

During the Civil War, people in Virginia disagreed.
People in western Virginia wanted to stay in the U.S.
People in eastern Virginia did not.
People in western Virginia formed a new state!

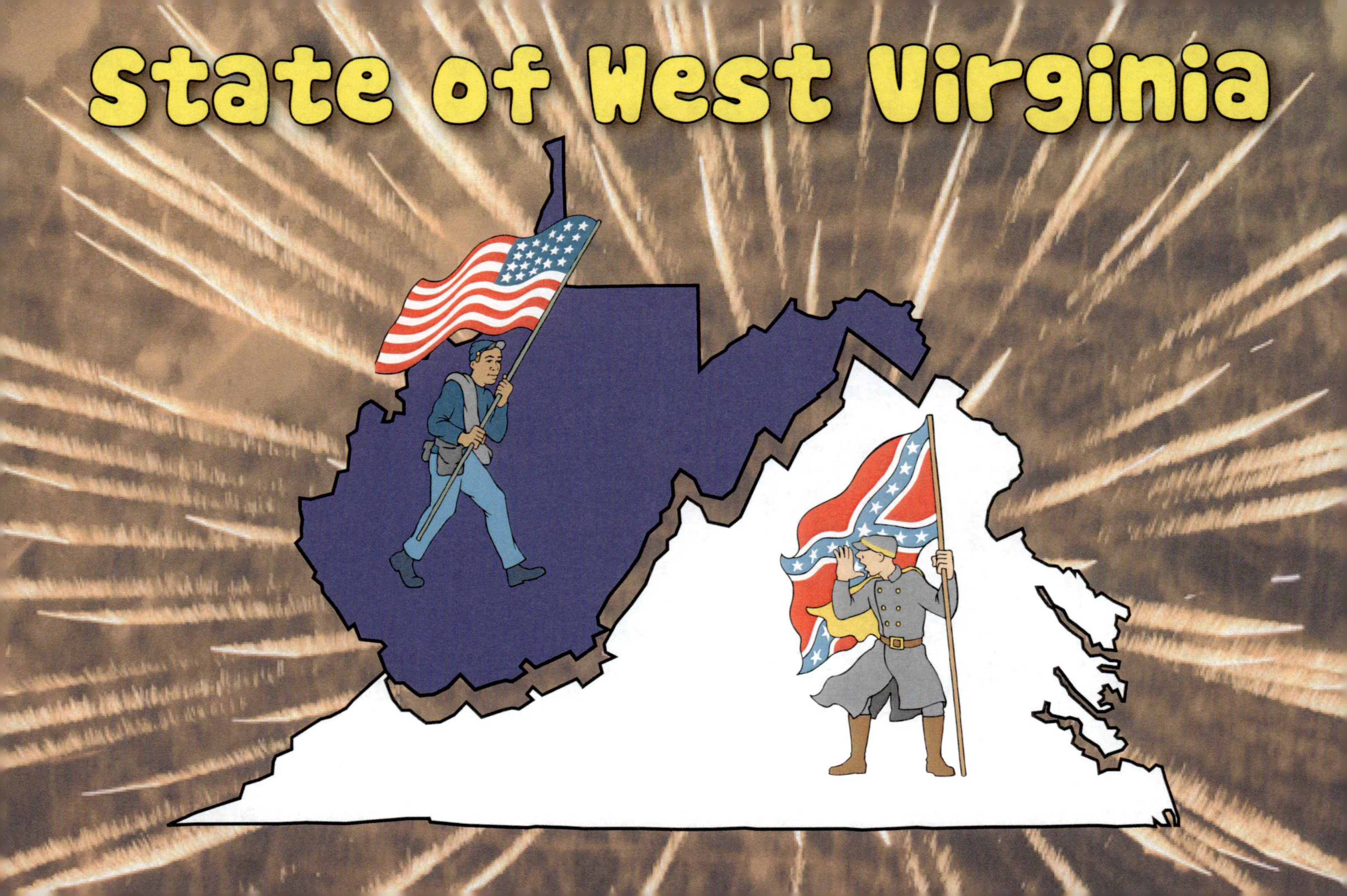
State of West Virginia

PEOPLE

Many famous people

Martin Robinson Delany

Doctor and newspaper editor who worked to end slavery

General Thomas "Stonewall" Jackson

Fought for the South during the Civil War

Booker T. Washington

African American teacher who improved education for blacks

Call our state home!

Chuck Yeager

Air Force test pilot who broke the sound barrier

Homer Hickam

Author of *Rocket Boys*, which was made into the movie *October Sky*

Mary Lou Retton

Gymnast who won five medals at the 1984 Olympics

Cardinal

BIRD

I am the state bird, and I fly
over West Virginia, proud and high.

As I fly, up in the sky,
I flap my wings to tell you "Hi!"

The West Virginia state bird is the Cardinal.

Rhododendron

FLOWER

I am the Rhododendron.
I am the state flower.

I grow where it's warm and sunny.
I bloom in spring and summer.
I help make West Virginia beautiful!

Look at me! Smell me!
But don't let animals eat my
leaves—they are poisonous!

Sugar Maple

TREE

I am a Sugar Maple—I'm the state tree.
All over West Virginia is where to find me.

My roots run deep, they keep me strong.
I can live for hundreds of years—that's very long!

I stand up straight, big and tall.
Don't climb too high—it would hurt to fall!

Honeybee

INSECT

I am the Honeybee.
I am the state insect.

I might sting you if you bother me,
But really, I am your friend.

I carry pollen from flower to flower.
I make honey.
I help West Virginia crops grow.

BZZZZZZZZZZ!

Rivers

RIVERS

West Virginia has many rivers.
People like to go white-water rafting on them!

The river habitat is home to many animals:

Birds **Deer** **Snakes** **Frogs** **Fish** **and More!**

Rivers were West Virginia's first highways.
People floated down the rivers on flatboats.
They carried goods to sell or trade!

Appalachian Mountains

MOUNTAINS

West Virginia's Appalachian Mountains
are the place to be.
Hiking, fishing, camping—
fun for you and me.

Winter weather brings lots of snow.
Temperatures drop to freezing and below!

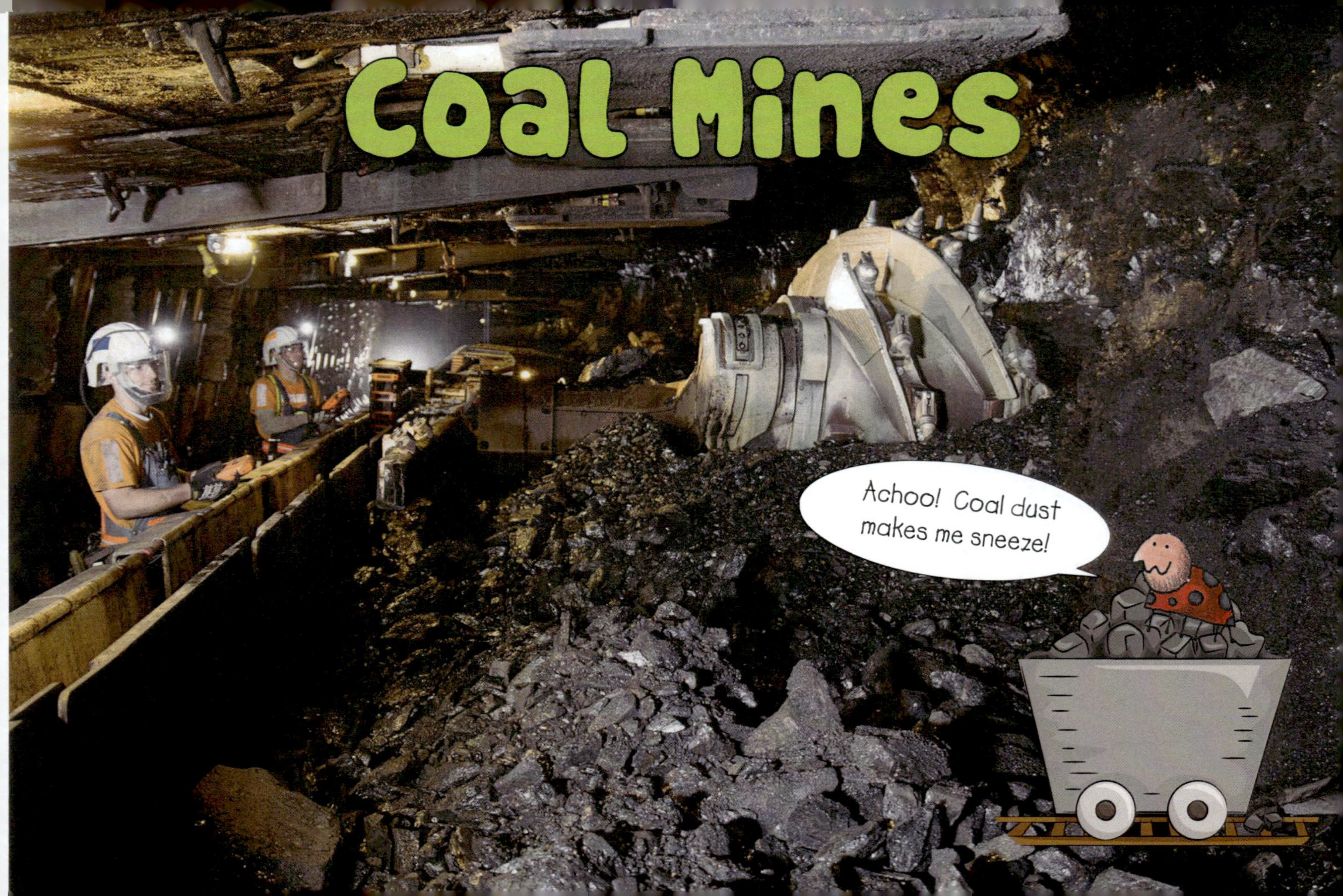
Coal Mines
Achoo! Coal dust makes me sneeze!

COALFIELDS

West Virginia has a valuable resource known as coal.
It is found deep under the ground.

Coal is very important to the world.
It is used to provide power for homes and businesses!

Bituminous coal is
West Virginia's state rock!

Let's fly down to the river.
You go first!
New River Gorge Bridge

LANDMARK

The New River Gorge Bridge crosses the New River.
It is one of the highest bridges in the United States.
When you travel across it,
you will see a beautiful view!

The bridge is a famous
West Virginia landmark.
Look for it on the West Virginia
state quarter!

West Virginia Crops

AGRICULTURE

West Virginia has many farms.
Why?
Because West Virginia has good soil
and a warm climate!

Some of the top crops grown in West Virginia are:

Hay Apples Corn Tobacco

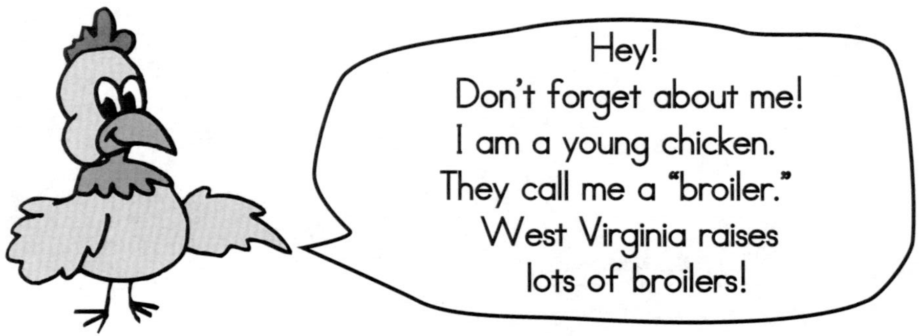

Sports in West Virginia

SPORTS

Baseball! Basketball! Football!
West Virginia has it all.

Whether you like to watch or play,
You are sure to have a ball!

Mountaineers

Thundering Herd

Yellow Jackets

& More!

West Virginia: Home of Golden Delicious apples

CLAIM TO FAME

Golden Delicious apples first came from West Virginia! The first tree was found about 100 years ago.

Golden Delicious apples are crisp, sweet, and juicy! They are good for making applesauce and apple juice.

The Golden Delicious apple is West Virginia's state fruit!

GLOSSARY

bituminous coal: black coal; the most common type of coal

broiler: a tender young chicken suitable for broiling (cooked under intense heat)

climate: weather conditions in an area over a long period of time

colony: a settlement ruled by another country

habitat: a place where plants or animals naturally live

laws: rules made by the government

poisonous: describes something that can cause death or illness if eaten

pollen: a yellow powder that helps plants make new plants

region: an area that has similar characteristics

settlement: the first community in an area